SELECTED
POEMS
DONALD
JUSTICE

SELECTED POEMS DONALD JUSTICE

NEW YORK ATHENEUM 1980

Some of the new poems in this book were published originally in *Antaeus, The New England Review, The Ohio Review,* and *The Sam Houston Literary Review.* The two *Tremayne* poems and two of the poems dealing with memories of the depression years (*Boston, Georgia* and *Miami, Florida*) first appeared in *The New Yorker.*

The Summer Anniversaries and *Night Light* were originally published by Wesleyan University Press, and the author wishes to thank that press for permission to include poems from those two volumes.

Thanks also to the Guggenheim Foundation and to the Corporation of Yaddo.

Poems from the following previously published books are included in the present volume of Selected Poems:

THE SUMMER ANNIVERSARIES, copyright © 1952, 1953, 1954, 1955, 1956, 1957, 1958, 1959, 1960 by Donald Justice

NIGHT LIGHT, copyright © 1961, 1962, 1963, 1964, 1965, 1966, 1967 by Donald Justice

DEPARTURES, copyright © 1969, 1970, 1971, 1972, 1973 by Donald Justice

Poems not previously published in book form are copyright © 1975, 1976, 1977, 1978, 1979 by Donald Justice

SELECTED POEMS copyright © 1979 by Donald Justice

All rights reserved

Published simultaneously in Canada by McClelland and Stewart Ltd

Library of Congress catalog card number 79-52416

ISBN 0-689-11016-2

Manufactured by American Book–Stratford Press, Saddle Brook, New Jersey

Designed by Harry Ford

First Printing November 1979

Second Printing April 1980

To the Memory of My Mother and Father

> *But ceasse worthy shepheard, nowe ceasse we to*
> *wery the hearers*
> *With monefull melodies, for enough our greefes*
> *be revealed,*
> *If by the parties ment our meanings rightly be marked,*
> *And sorrows do require some respitt unto the sences.*

Contents

DEPARTURES (1973)

UNCOLLECTED POEMS

FROM
THE SUMMER
ANNIVERSARIES

Ladies by Their Windows

1

They lean upon their windows. It is late.
Already it is twilight in the house;
Autumn is in their eyes. Twilit, autumnal—
Thus they regard themselves. What vanities!
As if all nature were a looking glass
To publish the small features of their ruin!

Each evening at their windows they arrive
As if in anticipation of farewells,
Though they would be still lingering if they could,
Weary, yet ever restless for the dance,
Old Cinderellas, hearing midnight strike,
The mouse-drawn coach impatient at the door.

2

The light in going still is golden, still
A single bird is singing in the wood,
Now one, now two, now three, and crickets start,
Bird-song and cricket-sigh; and all the small
Percussion of the grass booms as it can,
And chimes, and tinkles too, *fortissimo*.

It is the lurch and slur the world makes, turning.
It is the sound of turning, of a wheel
Or hand-cranked grinder turning, though more pomp
To this, more fiery particles struck off
At each revolve; and the last turn reveals
The darker side of what was light before.

Six stars shine through the dark, and half a moon!
Night birds go spiralling upwards with a flash
Of silvery underwings, silver ascendings,
The light of stars and of the moon their light.
And water lilies open to the moon,
The moon in wrinkles upon the water's face.

To shine is to be surrounded by the dark,
To glimmer in the very going out,

As stars wink, sinking in the bath of dawn,
Or as a prong of moon prolongs the night—
Superfluous curve!—unused to brilliancies
Which pale her own, yet splurging all she has.

3

So ladies by their windows live and die.
It is a question if they live or die,
As in a stone-wrought frieze of beasts and birds
The question is, whether they go or stay.
It seems they stay, but rest is motion too,
As these old mimicries of stone imply.

Say, then, they go by staying, bird and beast,
Still gathering momentum out of calm,
Till even stillness seems too much of haste
And haste too still. Say that they live by dying,
These who were warm and beautiful as summer,
Leaning upon their windows looking out,

Summer-surrounded then with leaf and vine,
With alternate sun and shade, these whom the noon
Wound once about with beauty and then unwound,
Whose warmth survives in coldness as of stone,
Beauty in shadows, action in lassitude,
Whose windows are the limits of their lives.

Women in Love

It always comes, and when it comes they know.
To will it is enough to take them there.
The knack is this, to fasten and not let go.

Their limbs are charmed; they cannot stay or go.
Desire is limbo—they're unhappy there.
It always comes, and when it comes they know.

Their choice of hells would be the one they know.
Dante describes it, the wind circling there.
The knack is this, to fasten and not let go.

The wind carries them where they want to go,
And that seems cruel to strangers passing there.
It always comes, and when it comes they know
The knack is this, to fasten and not let go.

Landscape with Little Figures

There were some pines, a canal, a piece of sky.
The pines are the houses now of the very poor,
Huddled together, in a blue, ragged wind.
Children go whistling their dogs, down by the mudflats,
Once the canal. There's a red ball lost in the weeds.
It's winter, it's after supper, it's goodbye.
O goodbye to the houses, the children, the little red ball,
And the pieces of sky that will go on falling for days.

In Bertram's Garden

Jane looks down at her organdy skirt
As if *it* somehow were the thing disgraced,
For being there, on the floor, in the dirt,
And she catches it up about her waist,
Smooths it out along one hip,
And pulls it over the crumpled slip.

On the porch, green-shuttered, cool,
Asleep is Bertram, that bronze boy,
Who, having wound her around a spool,
Sends her spinning like a toy
Out to the garden, all alone,
To sit and weep on a bench of stone.

Soon the purple dark will bruise
Lily and bleeding heart and rose,
And the little Cupid lose
Eyes and ears and chin and nose,
And Jane lie down with others soon
Naked to the naked moon.

Another Song

Merry the green, the green hill shall be merry.
Hungry, the owlet shall seek out the mouse,
And Jack his Joan, but they shall never marry.

And snows shall fly, the big flakes fat and furry.
Lonely, the traveler shall seek out the house,
And Jack his Joan, but they shall never marry.

Weary the soldiers go, and come back weary,
Up a green hill and down the withered hill,
And Jack from Joan, and they shall never marry.

Sonnet: The Poet at Seven

And on the porch, across the upturned chair,
The boy would spread a dingy counterpane
Against the length and majesty of the rain,
And on all fours crawl under it like a bear
To lick his wounds in secret, in his lair;
And afterwards, in the windy yard again,
One hand cocked back, release his paper plane
Frail as a May fly to the faithless air.
And summer evenings he would whirl around
Faster and faster till the drunken ground
Rose up to meet him; sometimes he would squat
Among the bent weeds of the vacant lot,
Waiting for dusk and someone dear to come
And whip him down the street, but gently, home.

Sonnet: The Wall

The walls surrounding them they never saw;
The angels, often. Angels were as common
As birds or butterflies, but looked more human.
As long as the wings were furled, they felt no awe.
Beasts, too, were friendly. They could find no flaw
In all of Eden: this was the first omen.
The second was the dream which woke the woman.
She dreamed she saw the lion sharpen his claw.
As for the fruit, it had no taste at all.
They had been warned of what was bound to happen.
They had been told of something called the world.
They had been told and told about the wall.
They saw it now; the gate was standing open.
As they advanced, the giant wings unfurled.

for John Berryman

10

A Winter Ode to the Old Men of Lummus Park, Miami, Florida

Risen from rented rooms, old ghosts
Come back to haunt our parks by day,
They creep up Fifth Street through the crowd,
Unseeing and almost unseen,
Halting before the shops for breath,
Still proud, pretending to admire
The fat hens dressed and hung for flies
There, or perhaps the lone, dead fern
Dressing the window of a small
Hotel. Winter has blown them south—
How many? Twelve in Lummus Park
I count now, shivering where they stand,
A little thicket of thin trees,
And more on benches turning with
The sun, wan heliotropes, all day.

O you who wear against the breast
The torturous flannel undervest
Winter and summer, yet are cold,
Poor cracked thermometers stuck now
At zero everlastingly,
Old men, bent like your walking sticks
As with the pressure of some hand,
Surely we must have thought you strong
To lean on you so hard, so long!

The Stray Dog by
the Summerhouse

This morning, down
By the summerhouse,
I saw a stray,
A stray dog dead.
All white and brown
The dead friend lay,
All brown with a white
Mark on his head.
His eyes were bright
And open wide,
Bright, open eyes
With worms inside,
And the tongue hung loose
To the butterflies,
The butterflies
And the flying ants.

And because of the tongue
He seemed like one
Who has run too long,
And stops, and pants.
And because of the sun
There came a scent,
And it was strong.
It came and went
As if somewhere near
A round, ripe pear,
So ripe, so round,
Had dropped to the ground
And with the heat
Was turning black.
And the scent came back,
And it was sweet.

On a Painting by Patient B of the Independence State Hospital for the Insane

WHO NAMED THE CLOUDS RABBIT, BEAR, AND HYENA

1

These seven houses have learned to face one another,
But not at the expected angles. Those silly brown lumps,
That are probably meant for hills and not other houses,
After ages of being themselves, though naturally slow,
Are learning to be exclusive without offending.
The arches and entrances (down to the right out of sight)
Have mastered the lesson of remaining closed.
And even the skies keep a certain understandable distance,
For these are the houses of the very rich.

2

One sees their children playing with leopards, tamed
At great cost, or perhaps it is only other children,
For none of these objects is anything more than a spot,
And perhaps there are not any children but only leopards
Playing with leopards, and perhaps there are only the spots.
And the little maids that hang from the windows like tongues,
Calling the children in, admiring the leopards,
Are the dashes a child might represent motion by means of,
Or dazzlement possibly, the brilliance of solid-gold houses.

3

The clouds resemble those empty balloons in cartoons
Which approximate silence. These clouds, if clouds they are
(And not the smoke from the seven aspiring chimneys),
The more one studies them the more it appears
They too have expressions. One might almost say
They have their habits, their wrong opinions, that their
Impassivity masks an essentially lovable foolishness,
And they will be given names by those who live under them
Not public like mountains' but private like companions'.

Counting the Mad

This one was put in a jacket,
This one was sent home,
This one was given bread and meat
But would eat none,
And this one cried No No No No
All day long.

This one looked at the window
As though it were a wall,
This one saw things that were not there,
This one things that were,
And this one cried No No No No
All day long.

This one thought himself a bird,
This one a dog,
And this one thought himself a man,
An ordinary man,
And cried and cried No No No No
All day long.

Beyond the Hunting Woods

I speak of that great house
Beyond the hunting woods,
Turreted and towered
In nineteenth-century style,
Where fireflies by the hundreds
Leap in the long grass,
Odor of jessamine
And roses, canker-bit,
Recalling famous times
When dame and maiden sipped
Sassafras or wild
Elderberry wine,
While far in the hunting woods
Men after their red hounds
Pursued the mythic beast.

I ask it of a stranger,
In all that great house finding
Not any living thing,
Or of the wind and the weather,
What charm was in that wine
That they should vanish so,
Ladies in their stiff
Bone and clean of limb,
And over the hunting woods
What mist had made them wild
That gentlemen should lose
Not only the beast in view
But Belle and Ginger too,
Nor home from the hunting woods
Ever, ever come?

Tales from a Family Album

How shall I speak of doom, and ours in special,
But as of something altogether common?
No house of Atreus ours, too humble surely,
The family tree a simple chinaberry
Such as springs up in Georgia in a season.
(Under it sags the farmer's broken wagon.)
Nor may I laud it much for shade or beauty,
But praise that tree for being prompt to flourish,
Despite the worm and weather out of heaven.

I publish of my folk how they have prospered
With something in the eyes, perhaps inherent,
Or great-winged nose, bespeaking an acquaintance
Not casual and not recent with a monster,
Citing, as an example of some courage,
That aunt, long gone, who kept one in a birdcage
Thirty-odd years in shape of a green parrot,
Nor overcame her fears, yet missed no feeding,
Thrust in the crumbs with thimbles on her fingers.

I had an uncle, long of arm and hairy,
Who seldom spoke in any lady's hearing
For fear his tongue should light on aught unseemly,
Yet he could treat most kindly with us children
Touching that beast, wholly imaginary,
Which, hunting once, his hounds had got the wind of.
And even of this present generation
There is a cousin of no great removal
On whom the mark is printed of a forepaw.

How shall I speak of doom and not the shadow
Caught in the famished cheeks of those few beauties
My people boast of, being flushed and phthisic?
Of my own childhood I remember dimly
One who died young, though as a hag most toothless,
Her fine hair wintry, from a hard encounter
By moonlight in a dark wood with a stranger,
Who had as well been unicorn or centaur
For all she might recall of him thereafter.

There was a kinsman took up pen and paper
To write our history, at which he perished,
Calling for water and the holy wafer,
Who had, till then, resisted all persuasion.
I pray your mercy on a leaf so shaken,
And mercy likewise on these other fallen,
Torn from the berry-tree in heaven's fashion,
For there was something in their way of going
Put doom upon my tongue and bade me utter.

Sestina: A Dream

I woke by first light in a wood
Right in the shadow of a hill
And saw about me in a circle
Many I knew, the dear faces
Of some I recognized as friends.
I knew that I had lost my way.

I asked if any knew the way.
They stared at me like blocks of wood.
They turned their backs on me, those friends,
And struggled up the stubborn hill
Along that road which makes a circle.
No longer could I see their faces.

But there were trees with human faces.
Afraid, I ran a little way
But must have wandered in a circle.
I had not left that human wood;
I was no farther up the hill.
And all the while I heard my friends

Discussing me, but not like friends.
Through gaps in trees I glimpsed their faces.
(The trees grow crooked on that hill.)
Now all at once I saw the way—
Above a clearing in the wood
A lone bird wheeling in a circle,

And in that shadowed space the circle
Of those I thought of still as friends.
I drew near, calling, and the wood
Rang and they turned their deaf faces
This way and that, but not my way.
They rose and stood upon the hill.

And it grew dark. Behind the hill
The sun slid down, a fiery circle;
Screeching, the bird flew on its way.
It was too dark to see my friends.

But then I saw them, and their faces
Were leaning above me like a wood.

Around me they circle on the hill.
But what is wrong with my friends' faces?
Why have they changed that way to wood?

Sestina: Here in Katmandu

We have climbed the mountain.
There's nothing more to do.
It is terrible to come down
To the valley
Where, amidst many flowers,
One thinks of snow,

As formerly, amidst snow,
Climbing the mountain,
One thought of flowers,
Tremulous, ruddy with dew,
In the valley.
One caught their scent coming down.

It is difficult to adjust, once down,
To the absence of snow.
Clear days, from the valley,
One looks up at the mountain.
What else is there to do?
Prayer wheels, flowers!

Let the flowers
Fade, the prayer wheels run down.
What have they to do
With us who have stood atop the snow
Atop the mountain,
Flags seen from the valley?

It might be possible to live in the valley,
To bury oneself among flowers,
If one could forget the mountain,
How, never once looking down,
Stiff, blinded with snow,
One knew what to do.

Meanwhile it is not easy here in Katmandu,
Especially when to the valley
That wind which means snow
Elsewhere, but here means flowers,
Comes down,
As soon it must, from the mountain.

Anthony Street

1

Morning. The roofs emerge, the yard—
Brown grass, puddled with snow, dog's bone—
Emerges slowly, but not yet
Her plumber from the widow's arms
To touch his dreaming truck awake
That all night slumbered by our curb,
Nor yet the lame child from his race,
His dog from rat and squirrel. Only,
At the horizon now, dark pines
Scatter their starlings to the wires.

2

Evening. The paper-boy on wheels
Turns at his corner into night.
The one-armed man, returning late,
Bends to retrieve the murderous news,
Tucks it beneath the willing stump,
And mounts once more with slippery care
The purgatory of the stoop.
Withindoors many now enact,
Behind drawn shades, their shadow lives.
The headlights, turning, grope their way.

On the Death of Friends in Childhood

We shall not ever meet them bearded in heaven,
Nor sunning themselves among the bald of hell;
If anywhere, in the deserted schoolyard at twilight,
Forming a ring, perhaps, or joining hands
In games whose very names we have forgotten.
Come, memory, let us seek them there in the shadows.

The Snowfall

The classic landscapes of dreams are not
More pathless, though footprints leading nowhere
Would seem to prove that a people once
Survived for a little even here.

Fragments of a pathetic culture
Remain, the lost mittens of children,
And a single, bright, detasseled snow cap,
Evidence of some frantic migration.

The landmarks are gone. Nevertheless,
There is something familiar about this country.
Slowly now we begin to recall

The terrible whispers of our elders
Falling softly about our ears
In childhood, never believed till now.

A Map of Love

Your face more than others' faces
Maps the half-remembered places
I have come to while I slept—
Continents a dream had kept
Secret from all waking folk
Till to your face I awoke,
And remembered then the shore,
And the dark interior.

FROM
NIGHT LIGHT

Heart

Heart, let us this once reason together.
Thou art a child no longer. Only think
What sport the neighbors have from us, not without cause.
These nightly sulks, these clamorous demonstrations!
Already they tell of thee a famous story.
An antique, balding spectacle such as thou art,
Affecting still that childish, engaging stammer
With all the seedy innocence of an overripe pomegranate!
Henceforth, let us conduct ourselves more becomingly!

And still I hear thee, beating thy little fist
Against the walls. My dear, have I not led thee,
Dawn after streaky dawn, besotted, home?
And still these threats to have off as before?
From thee, who wouldst lose thyself in the next street?
Go then, O my inseparable, this once more.
Afterwards we will take thought for our good name.

Time and the Weather

Time and the weather wear away
The houses that our fathers built.
Their ghostly furniture remains—
All the sad sofas we have stained
With tears of boredom and of guilt,

The fraying mottoes, the stopped clocks . . .
And still sometimes these tired shapes
Haunt the damp parlors of the heart.
What Sunday prisons they recall!
And what miraculous escapes!

Ode to a Dressmaker's Dummy

*Papier-maché body; blue-and-black cotton
jersey cover. Metal stand. Instructions included.*
SEARS, ROEBUCK CATALOGUE

O my coy darling, still
You wear for me the scent
Of those long afternoons we spent,
The two of us together,
Safe in the attic from the jealous eyes
Of household spies
And the remote buffooneries of the weather;
So high,
Our sole remaining neighbor was the sky,
Which, often enough, at dusk,
Leaning her cloudy shoulders on the sill,
Used to regard us with a bored and cynical eye.

How like the terrified,
Shy figure of a bride
You stood there then, without your clothes,
Drawn up into
So classic and so strict a pose
Almost, it seemed, our little attic grew
Dark with the first charmed night of the honeymoon.
Or was it only some obscure
Shape of my mother's youth I saw in you,
There where the rude shadows of the afternoon
Crept up your ankles and you stood
Hiding your sex as best you could?—
Prim ghost the evening light shone through.

The Grandfathers

Why will they never sleep?
JOHN PEALE BISHOP

Why will they never sleep,
The old ones, the grandfathers?
Always you find them sitting
On ruined porches, deep
In the back country, at dusk,
Hawking and spitting.
They might have sat there forever,
Tapping their sticks,
Peevish, discredited gods.
Ask the lost traveler how,
At road-end, they will fix
You maybe with the cold
Eye of a snake or a bird
And answer not a word,
Only these blank, oracular
Headshakes or headnods.

Anonymous Drawing

A delicate young Negro stands
With the reins of a horse clutched loosely in his hands;
So delicate, indeed, that we wonder if he can hold the spirited
        creature beside him
Until the master shall arrive to ride him.
Already the animal's nostrils widen with rage or fear.
But if we imagine him snorting, about to rear,
This boy, who should know about such things better than we,
Only stands smiling, passive and ornamental, in a fantastic livery
Of ruffles and puffed breeches,
Watching the artist, apparently, as he sketches.
Meanwhile the petty lord who must have paid
For the artist's trip up from Perugia, for the horse, for the boy, for
        everything here, in fact, has been delayed,
Kept too long by his steward, perhaps, discussing
Some business concerning the estate, or fussing
Over the details of his impeccable toilet
With a manservant whose opinion is that any alteration at all would
        spoil it.
However fast he should come hurrying now
Over this vast greensward, mopping his brow
Clear of the sweat of the fine Renaissance morning, it would be too
        late.
The artist will have had his revenge for being made to wait,
A revenge not only necessary but right and clever—
Simply to leave him out of the scene forever.

Variations for Two Pianos

There is no music now in all Arkansas.
Higgins is gone, taking both his pianos.

Movers dismantled the instruments, away
Sped the vans. The first detour untuned the strings.
There is no music now in all Arkansas.

Up Main Street, past the cold shopfronts of Conway,
The brash, self-important brick of the college,
Higgins is gone, taking both his pianos.

Warm evenings, the windows open, he would play
Something of Mozart's for his pupils, the birds.
There is no music now in all Arkansas.

How shall the mockingbird mend her trill, the jay
His eccentric attack, lacking a teacher?
Higgins is gone, taking both his pianos.

There is no music now in all Arkansas.

for Thomas Higgins, pianist

But That Is Another Story

I do not think the ending can be right.
How can they marry and live happily
Forever, these who were so passionate
At chapter's end? Once they are settled in
The quiet country house, what will they do,
So many miles from anywhere?
Those blond Victorian ghosts crowding the stair,
Surely they disapprove? Ah me,
I fear love will catch cold and die
From pacing naked through those drafty halls
Night after night. Poor Frank! Poor Imogene!
Before them now their lives
Stretch empty as great Empire beds
After the lovers rise and the damp sheets
Are stripped by envious chambermaids.

And if the first night passes brightly enough,
What with the bonfires built of old love letters,
That is no inexhaustible fuel, I think.
A later dusk may find them, hand in hand,
Stopping among the folds to watch
The mating of the more ebullient sheep.
(And yet how soon the wool itself must lie
Scattered like snow, or miniature fallen clouds.)
God knows how it will end, not I.
Will Frank walk out one day
Alone through the ruined orchard with his stick,
Strewing the path with lissome heads
Of buttercups? Will Imogene
Conceal in the hollows of appointed oaks
Love notes for beardless gardeners and the like?

Meanwhile they quarrel, and make it up,
Only to quarrel again. A sudden storm
Pulls the last fences down. The stupid sheep
Stand out all night now coughing in the garden
And peering through the windows where they sleep.

Last Days of Prospero

The aging magician retires to his island.
It is not so green as he remembers,
Nor does the sea caress its headlands
With the customary nuptial music.

He does not mind. He will not mind,
So long as the causeway to the island
Is not repaired, so long as the gay little
Tourist steamer never again

Lurches late into harbor, and no one
Applies for a license to reopen
The shuttered, pink casino. Better,
He thinks, an isle unvisited

Except for the sea birds come to roost
On the roofs of the thousand ruined cabañas,
Survivors, or the strayed whale, offshore,
Suspicious, surfacing to spout,

Noble as any fountain of Mílan . . .
The cave? That is as he had left it,
Amply provisioned against the days
To come. His cloak? Neat on its hanger;

The painted constellations, though faded
With damp a little, still glitter
And seem in the dark to move on course.
His books? He knows where they were drowned.

(What tempests he had caused, what lightnings
Loosed in the rigging of the world!)
If now it is all to be started up
Again, nothing lacks to his purpose.

Some change in the wording of the charm,
Some slight reshuffling of negative
And verb, perhaps—that should suffice.
But meanwhile he will pace the strand,

Debating, as old men will, with himself
Or with the waves, and still the waves
Come back at him always with the same
Low chucklings or grand, indifferent sighs.

After a Phrase Abandoned
by Wallace Stevens

The alp at the end of the street
STEVENS' NOTEBOOKS

The alp at the end of the street
Occurs in the dreams of the town.
Over burgher and shopkeeper,
Massive, he broods,
A snowy-headed father
Upon whose knees his children
No longer climb;
Or is reflected
In the cool, unruffled lakes of
Their minds, at evening,
After their day in the shops,
As shadow only, shapeless
As a wind that has stopped blowing.

Grandeur, it seems,
Comes down to this in the end—
A street of shops
With white shutters
Open for business . . .

The Suicides

If we recall your voices
As softer now, it's only
That they must have drifted back

A long way to have reached us
Here, and upon such a wind
As crosses the high passes.

Nor does the blue of your eyes
(Remembered) cast much light on
The page ripped from the tablet.

———

Once there in the labyrinth,
You were safe from your reasons.
We stand, now, at the threshold,

Peering in, but the passage,
For us, remains obscure; the
Corridors are still bloody.

———

What you meant to prove you have
Proved—we did not care for you
Nearly enough. Meanwhile the

Bay was preparing herself
To receive you, the for once
Wholly adequate female

To your dark inclinations;
Under your care the pistol
Was slowly learning to flower

In the desired explosion,
Disturbing the careful part
And the briefly recovered

Fixed smile of a forgotten
Triumph; deep within the black
Forest of childhood that tree

Was already rising which,
With the length of your body,
Would cast the double shadow.

———

The masks by which we knew you
Have been torn from you. Even
Those mirrors, to which always

You must have turned to confide,
Cannot have recognized you,
Stripped, as you were, finally.

At the end of your shadow
There sat another, waiting,
Whose back was always to us.

———

When the last door had been closed,
You watched, inwardly raging,
For the first glimpse of your selves
Approaching, jangling their keys.

Musicians of the black keys,
At last you compose yourselves.
We hear the music raging
Under the lids we have closed.

in memory of J. and G. and J.

Orpheus Opens His Morning Mail

Bills. Bills. From the mapmakers of hell, the repairers of fractured
lutes, the bribed judges of musical contests, etc.

A note addressed to my wife, marked: *Please Forward.*

A group photograph, signed: *Your Admirers.* In their faces a certain
sameness, as if "1" might, after all, be raised to some modest
power; likewise in their costumes, at once transparent and
identical, like those of young ladies at some debauched
seminary. Already—such is my weakness—I picture the rooms
into which they must once have locked themselves to read my
work: those barren cells, beds ostentatiously unmade; the
single pinched chrysanthemum, memorializing in a corner
some withered event; the mullioned panes, high up, through
which may be spied, far off, the shorn hedge behind which a
pimply tomorrow crouches, exposing himself. O lassitudes!

Finally, an invitation to attend certain rites to be celebrated, come
equinox, on the river bank. I am to be guest of honor. As
always, I rehearse the scene in advance: the dark; the guards,
tipsy as usual, sonorously snoring; a rustling, suddenly,
among the reeds; the fitful illumination of ankles, whitely
flashing . . . Afterwards, I shall probably be asked to recite
my poems. But O my visions, my vertigoes! Have I imagined
it only, the perverse gentility of their shrieks?

To the Unknown Lady Who
Wrote the Letters Found
in the Hatbox

To be sold at auction: . . . 1 brass bed, 1
walnut secretary . . . birdcages, a hatbox of
old letters . . . NEWSPAPER ADVERTISEMENT

What, was there never any news?
And were your weathers always fine,
Your colds all common, and your blues
Too minor to deserve one line?

Between the lines it must have hurt
To see the neighborhood go down,
Your neighbor in his undershirt
At dusk come out to mow his lawn.

But whom to turn to to complain
Unless it might be your canaries,
And only in bird language then?
While slowly into mortuaries

The many-storied houses went
Or in deep, cataracted eyes
Displayed their signs of want—FOR RENT
And MADAM ROXIE WILL ADVISE.

The Evening of the Mind

Now comes the evening of the mind.
Here are the fireflies twitching in the blood;
Here is the shadow moving down the page
Where you sit reading by the garden wall.
Now the dwarf peach trees, nailed to their trellises,
Shudder and droop. You know their voices now,
Faintly the martyred peaches crying out
Your name, the name nobody knows but you.
It is the aura and the coming on.
It is the thing descending, circling, here.
And now it puts a claw out and you take it.
Thankfully in your lap you take it, so.

You said you would not go away again,
You did not want to go away—and yet,
It is as if you stood out on the dock
Watching a little boat drift out
Beyond the sawgrass shallows, the dead fish . . .
And you were in it, skimming past old snags,
Beyond, beyond, under a brazen sky
As soundless as a gong before it's struck—
Suspended how?—and now they strike it, now
The ether dream of five-years-old repeats, repeats,
And you must wake again to your own blood
And empty spaces in the throat.

Dreams of Water

1

An odd silence
Falls as we enter
The cozy ship's-bar.

The captain, smiling,
Unfolds his spyglass
And offers to show you

The obscene shapes
Of certain islands,
Low in the offing.

I sit by in silence.

2

People in raincoats
Stand looking out from
Ends of piers.

A fog gathers;
And little tugs,
Growing uncertain

Of their position,
Start to complain
With the deep and bearded

Voices of fathers.

3

The season is ending.
White verandas
Curve away.

The hotel seems empty
But, once inside,
I hear a great splashing.

Behind doors
Grandfathers loll
In steaming tubs,

Huge, unblushing.

Early Poems

How fashionably sad those early poems are!
On their clipped lawns and hedges the snows fall.
Rains beat against the tarpaulins of their porches,
Where, Sunday mornings, the bored children sprawl,
Reading the comics before their parents rise.
—The rhymes, the meters, how they paralyze.

Who walks out through their streets tonight? No one.
You know these small towns, how all traffic stops
At ten. Idly, the street lamps gather moths,
And the pale mannequins wait inside dark shops,
Undressed, and ready for the dreams of men.
—Now the long silence. Now the beginning again.

American Sketches

CROSSING KANSAS BY TRAIN

The telephone poles
Have been holding their
Arms out
A long time now
To birds
That will not
Settle there
But pass with
Strange cawings
Westward to
Where dark trees
Gather about a
Waterhole this
Is Kansas the
Mountains start here
Just behind
The closed eyes
Of a farmer's
Sons asleep
In their workclothes

POEM TO BE READ AT 3 A.M.

Excepting the diner
On the outskirts
The town of Ladora
At 3 A.M.
Was dark but
For my headlights
And up in
One second-story room
A single light
Where someone
Was sick or
Perhaps reading
As I drove past
At seventy
Not thinking
This poem
Is for whoever
Had the light on

for William Carlos Williams

Memory of a Porch

MIAMI, 1942

What I remember
Is how the wind chime
Commenced to stir
As she spoke of her childhood,

As though the simple
Death of a pet cat,
Buried with flowers,

Had brought to the porch
A rumor of storms
Dying out over
Some dark Atlantic.

At least I heard
The thing begin—
A thin, skeletal music—

And in the deep silence
Below all memory
The sighing of ferns
Half asleep in their boxes.

Bus Stop

Lights are burning
In quiet rooms
Where lives go on
Resembling ours.

The quiet lives
That follow us—
These lives we lead
But do not own—

Stand in the rain
So quietly
When we are gone,
So quietly . . .

And the last bus
Comes letting dark
Umbrellas out—
Black flowers, black flowers.

And lives go on.
And lives go on
Like sudden lights
At street corners

Or like the lights
In quiet rooms
Left on for hours,
Burning, burning.

In the Greenroom

How reassuring
To discover them
In the greenroom. Here,

Relaxing, they drop
The patronymics
By which we had come

To know them. The cross
Are no longer cross,
The old dance, nor have

The young sacrificed
Their advantages.
In this it is like

A kind of heaven
They rise to simply
By being themselves.

The sound of the axe
Biting the wood is
Rewound on the tape.

Nothing has happened.
What is this green for,
If not renewal?

At a Rehearsal of Uncle Vanya

NURSE: *The crows might get them.*

You mean well, doctor,
But are—forgive me—
A bit of a crank,

A friend they may love
But cannot listen
To long, for yawning.

When you are gone, though,
They move up close to
The stove's great belly.

Yes, they are burning
Your forests, doctor,
The dark green forests.

There is a silence
That falls between them
Like snow, like deep snow.

Horses have gone lame
Crossing the waste lands
Between two people.

We hear the old nurse
Calling her chickens
In now: *chook chook chook.*

It's cold in Russia.
We sit here, doctor,
In the crows' shadow.

San Francisco, Actor's Workshop, December, 1964

To the Hawks

McNamara, Rusk, Bundy, etc.

Farewell is the bell
Beginning to ring.

The children singing
Do not yet hear it.

The sun is shining
In their song. The sun

Is in fact shining
Upon the schoolyard,

On children swinging
Like tongues of a bell

Swung out on the long
Arc of a silence

That will not seem to
Have been a silence

Till it is broken,
As it is breaking.

There is a sun now
Louder than the sun

Of which the children
Are singing, brighter,

Too, than that other
Against whose brightness

Their eyes seem caught in
The act of shutting.

The young schoolteacher,
Waving one arm in

Time to the music,
Is waving farewell.

Her mouth is open
To sound the alarm.

The mouth of the world
Grows round with the sound.

February, 1965

The Tourist from Syracuse

*One of those men who can be a car salesman
or a tourist from Syracuse or a hired assassin.*
JOHN D. MACDONALD

You would not recognize me.
Mine is the face which blooms in
The dank mirrors of washrooms
As you grope for the light switch.

My eyes have the expression
Of the cold eyes of statues
Watching their pigeons return
From the feed you have scattered,

And I stand on my corner
With the same marble patience.
If I move at all, it is
At the same pace precisely

As the shade of the awning
Under which I stand waiting
And with whose blackness it seems
I am already blended.

I speak seldom, and always
In a murmur as quiet
As that of crowds which surround
The victims of accidents.

Shall I confess who I am?
My name is all names, or none.
I am the used-car salesman,
The tourist from Syracuse,

The hired assassin, waiting.
I will stand here forever
Like one who has missed his bus—
Familiar, anonymous—

55

On my usual corner,
The corner at which you turn
To approach that place where now
You must not hope to arrive.

The Man Closing Up

1
Like a deserted beach,
The man closing up.

Broken glass on the rocks,
And seaweed coming in
To hang up on the rocks.

Old pilings, rotted, broken like teeth,
Where a pier was,

A mouth,
And the tide coming in.

The man closing up
Is like this.

2
He has no hunger
For anything,
The man closing up.

He would even try stones,
If they were offered.

But he has no hunger
For stones.

3
He would make his bed,
If he could sleep on it.

He would make his bed with white sheets
And disappear into the white,

Like a man diving,
If he could be certain

That the light
Would not keep him awake,

The light that reaches
To the bottom.

4
The man closing up
Tries the doors.

But first
He closes the windows.

And before that even
He had looked out the windows.

There was no storm coming
That he could see.

There was no one out walking
At that hour.

Still,
He closes the windows
And tries the doors.

He knows about storms
And about people

And about hours
Like that one.

5

There is a word for it,
A simple word,
And the word goes around.

It curves like a staircase,
And it goes up like a staircase,
And it *is* a staircase,

An iron staircase
On the side of a lighthouse.
All in his head.

And it makes no sound at all
In his head,
Unless he says it.

Then the keeper
Steps on the rung,
The bottom rung,

And the ascent begins.
Clangorous,
Rung after rung.

He wants to keep the light going,
If he can.

But the man closing up
Does not say the word.

improvisations on themes from Guillevic

Men at Forty

Men at forty
Learn to close softly
The doors to rooms they will not be
Coming back to.

At rest on a stair landing,
They feel it
Moving beneath them now like the deck of a ship,
Though the swell is gentle.

And deep in mirrors
They rediscover
The face of the boy as he practices tying
His father's tie there in secret

And the face of that father,
Still warm with the mystery of lather.
They are more fathers than sons themselves now.
Something is filling them, something

That is like the twilight sound
Of the crickets, immense,
Filling the woods at the foot of the slope
Behind their mortgaged houses.

The Missing Person

He has come to report himself
A missing person.

The authorities
Hand him the forms.

He knows how they have waited
With the learned patience of barbers

In small shops, idle,
Stropping their razors.

But now that these spaces in his life
Stare up at him blankly,

Waiting to be filled in,
He does not know how to begin.

Afraid that he may not answer
To his description of himself,

He asks for a mirror.
They reassure him

That he can be nowhere
But wherever he finds himself

From moment to moment,
Which, for the moment, is here.

And he might like to believe them.
But in the mirror

He sees what is missing.
It is himself

He sees there emerging
Slowly, as from the dark

Of a furnished room
Only by darkness,

One who receives no mail
And is known to the landlady only

For keeping himself to himself,
And for whom it will be years yet

Before he can trust to the light
This last disguise, himself.

Elsewheres

SOUTH

The long green shutters are drawn.
Against what parades?

Closing our eyes against the sun,
We try to imagine

The darkness of an interior
Where something might still happen:

The razor lying open
On the cool marble washstand,

The drip of something—is it water?—
Upon stone floors.

NORTH

Already it is midsummer
In the Sweden of our lives.

The peasants have joined hands,
They are circling the haystacks.

We watch from the veranda.
We sit, mufflered,

Humming the tune in snatches
Under our breath.

We tremble sometimes,
Not with emotion.

Reading the signs,
We learn what to expect—

The trains late,
The machines out of order.

We learn what it is
To stare out into space.

Great farms surround us,
Squares of a checkerboard.

Taking our places, we wait,
We wait to be moved.

Incident in a Rose Garden

The gardener came running,
An old man, out of breath.
Fear had given him legs.
> Sir, I encountered Death
> Just now among the roses.
> Thin as a scythe he stood there.
> I knew him by his pictures.
> He had his black coat on,
> Black gloves, a broad black hat.
> I think he would have spoken,
> Seeing his mouth stood open.
> Big it was, with white teeth.
> As soon as he beckoned, I ran.
> I ran until I found you.
> Sir, I am quitting my job.
> I want to see my sons
> Once more before I die.
> I want to see California.
We shook hands; he was off.

And there stood Death in the garden,
Dressed like a Spanish waiter.
He had the air of someone
Who because he likes arriving
At all appointments early
Learns to think himself patient.
I watched him pinch one bloom off
And hold it to his nose—
A connoisseur of roses—
One bloom and then another.
They strewed the earth around him.
> Sir, you must be that stranger
> Who threatened my gardener.
> This is my property, sir.
> I welcome only friends here.

Death grinned, and his eyes lit up
With the pale glow of those lanterns
That workmen carry sometimes
To light their way through the dusk.
Now with great care he slid
The glove from his right hand
And held that out in greeting,
A little cage of bone.

> *Sir, I knew your father,*
> *And we were friends at the end.*
> *As for your gardener,*
> *I did not threaten him.*
> *Old men mistake my gestures.*
> *I only meant to ask him*
> *To show me to his master.*
> *I take it you are he?*

for Mark Strand

The Thin Man

I indulge myself
In rich refusals.
Nothing suffices.

I hone myself to
This edge. Asleep, I
Am a horizon.

Hands

Les mains ne trouvaient plus
De bonheur dans les poches.
GUILLEVIC

No longer do the hands know
The happiness of pockets.

Sometimes they hang at the sides
Like the dead weights of a clock.

Sometimes they clench into fists
Around the neck of anger.

Formerly there were brothers
To clasp, shoulders to rest on.

If now they unfold like maps,
All their countries seem foreign.

They dream of returning to
The dark home of the pockets.

They want to wash themselves clean
Of the blood of old salutes,

To scrub away the perfumes
Of the flesh they have tasted.

And all that they grasp is air.
Think of the hands as breathing,

Opening, closing. Think of
The emptiness of the hands.

To Waken a Small Person

You sleep at the top of streets
Up which workmen each morning
Go wheeling their bicycles

Your eyes are like the windows
Of some high attic the one
The very one you sleep in

They're shut it's raining the rain
Falls on the streets of the town
As it falls through your sleep stop

You must be dreaming these tears
Wake up please open yourself
Like a little umbrella

Hurry the sidewalks need you
The awnings not one is up
And the patient bicycles

Halted at intersections
They need you they are confused
The colors of traffic lights

Are bleeding bleeding wake up
The puddles of parking lots
Cannot contain such rainbows

FROM
DEPARTURES

Fragment: To a Mirror

Behind that bland facade of yours,
What drafts are moving down what intricate maze
Of halls? What solitude of attics waits,
Bleak, at the top of the still hidden stair?
And are these windows yours that open out
On such spectacular views?
Those still bays yours, where small boats lie
At anchor, abandoned by their crews?
The parks nearby,
Whose statues doze forever in the sun?
Those stricken avenues,
Along which great palms wither and droop down
Their royal fronds,
And the parade is drummed
To a sudden inexplicable halt?
                              Tell me,
Is this the promised absence I foresee
In you, where no breath any more shall stir
The surface of the sleeping pond,
And you shall have back your rest at last,
Your half of nothingness?

1963–1972

73

Things

Hard, but you can polish it.
Precious, it has eyes. Can wound.
Would dance upon water. Sinks.
Stays put. Crushed, becomes a road.

(STONE)

Mine to give, mine to offer
No resistance. Mine
To receive you, mine to keep
The shape of our nights.

(PILLOW)

My former friend, my traitor.
My too easily broken.
My still to be escaped from.

(MIRROR)

To support this roof.
To stand up. To take
Such weight in the knees . . .
To keep the secret.
To envy no cloud.

(WALL)

74

Two Small Vices Beginning with the Letter "L"

LETHARGY

It smiles to see me
Still in my bathrobe.

It sits in my lap
And will not let me rise.

Now it is kissing my eyes.
Arms enfold me, arms

Pale with a thick down.
It seems I am falling asleep

To the sound of a story
Being read me.

This is the story.
Weeks have passed

Since first I lifted my hand
To set it down.

LUXURY

You are like a sun of the tropics
Peering through blinds

Drawn for siesta.
Already you teach me

The Spanish for sunflower.
Such iridescence!

You, alone on the clean sheet,
Unadorned.

You, like the spilt moon.
You, like a star

Hidden by sun-goggles.
You shall have a thousand lovers.

You, spread here like butter,
Like doubloons, like flowers.

A Dancer's Life

The lights in the theater fail. The long racks
Of costumes abandoned by the other dancers
Trouble Celeste. The conductor asks
If she is sad because autumn is coming on,

But when autumn comes she is merely pregnant and bored.
On her way back from the holidays, a man
Who appears to have no face rattles the door
To her compartment. *How disgusting*, she thinks;

How disgusting it always must be to grow old.
Dusk falls, and a few drops of rain.
On the train window trembles the blurred
Reflection of her own transparent beauty,

And through this, beautiful ruined cities passing,
Dark forests, and people everywhere
Pacing on lighted platforms, some
Beating their children, some apparently dancing.

The costumes of the dancers sway in the chill darkness.
Now sinking into sleep is like sinking again
Into the lake of her youth. Her parents
Lean from the rail of a ferryboat waving, waving,

As the boat glides farther out across the waves.
No one, it seems, is meeting her at the station.
The city is frozen. She warms herself
In the pink and scented twilight of a bar.

The waiter who serves her is young. She nods assent.
The conversation dies in bed. Later,
She hurries off to rehearsal. In the lobby,
Dizzy still with the weight of her own body,

She waits, surrounded by huge stills of herself
And bright posters announcing events to come.
Her life—she feels it closing about her now
Like a small theater, empty, without lights.

The Confession

You have no name, intimate crime;
There is nothing to whisper.
You have fled across many pillows,
But you leave nothing behind.

Dressed in the silence you were sworn to,
You passed without recognition.
No door holds you, no mirror;
I am the lone witness.

You have escaped into smoke,
Into the dark mouths of tunnels.
Once in the streets you were safe,
You were one among many.

The Success

He asks for directions, but the street
Is swaying before him drunkenly.
The buildings lean together. There is some
Conspiracy of drawn curtains against him.

And all around him he can sense the beauty
Of unseen arms, of eyes that slide off elsewhere.
Someone is living his life here, someone
Is turning back sheets meant to receive his body.

This is the address if not the destination.
The moonlight dies along his wrist. His hand
Slips off through the darkness on its stubborn mission,
Roving the row of mailboxes for the name it dreams.

He enters. The doorman vanishes with a nod.
The elevator ascends smoothly to his desire.
The light in the hall, the door against his cheek . . .
He has arrived. He recognizes the laughter.

The Assassination

It begins again, the nocturnal pulse.
It courses through the cables laid for it.
It mounts to the chandeliers and beats there, hotly.
We are too close. Too late, we would move back.
We are involved with the surge.

Now it bursts. Now it has been announced.
Now it is being soaked up by newspapers.
Now it is running through the streets.
The crowd has it. The woman selling carnations
And the man in the straw hat stand with it in their shoes.

Here is the red marquee it sheltered under,
Here is the ballroom, here
The sadly various orchestra led
By a single gesture. My arms open.
It enters. Look, we are dancing.

June 5, 1968

Twenty Questions

Is it raining out?
Is it raining in?
Are you a public fountain?
Are you an antique musical instrument?
Are you a famous resort, perhaps?
What is your occupation?
Are you by chance a body of water?
Do you often travel alone?
What is your native language, then?
Do you recall the word for carnation?

Are you sorry?
Will you be sorry?
Is this your handkerchief?
What is your destination?
Are you Aquarius?
Are you the watermelon flower?
Will you please take off your glasses?
Is this a holiday for you?
Is that a scar, or a birthmark?
Is there no word for calyx in your tongue?

Poem

This poem is not addressed to you.
You may come into it briefly,
But no one will find you here, no one.
You will have changed before the poem will.

Even while you sit there, unmovable,
You have begun to vanish. And it does not matter.
The poem will go on without you.
It has the spurious glamor of certain voids.

It is not sad, really, only empty.
Once perhaps it was sad, no one knows why.
It prefers to remember nothing.
Nostalgias were peeled from it long ago.

Your type of beauty has no place here.
Night is the sky over this poem.
It is too black for stars.
And do not look for any illumination.

You neither can nor should understand what it means.
Listen, it comes without guitar,
Neither in rags nor any purple fashion.
And there is nothing in it to comfort you.

Close your eyes, yawn. It will be over soon.
You will forget the poem, but not before
It has forgotten you. And it does not matter.
It has been most beautiful in its erasures.

O bleached mirrors! Oceans of the drowned!
Nor is one silence equal to another.
And it does not matter what you think.
This poem is not addressed to you.

Portraits of the Sixties

1 PORTRAIT WITH SHORT HAIR

The days, the days!
And the scissors you cut
Your hair with—oh, how dull.
Time to change the needle.

Put on another record—
No, something baroque—
And think of the good times.
Think of lakes and rivers.

It's hot. Let in some air.
Let the smell of leftovers
Be one with the perfume
Of cooling asphalt, leaves.

And the nights? Ah, wonderful—
You alone,
Alone with the slums,
The flowerpots, the stars.

Think of the sea. Unzip,
Just as though someone were
Around to be made love to,
Or anyway to pose for.

The mysteries of sex!
Some day you'll wake up
Back on that Christmas morning
In Mexico, still a virgin.

What lonely aisles you prowled
In search of the forbidden,
Blinking your usher's torch,
Firefly of the balconies!

And when you found it—love!—
It was to pure French horns
Soaring above the plains
Of Saturday's Westerns.

The defiant eyes laughing
Into the sudden beam,
The soft Mexican curses,
The stains, the crushed corsages . . .

Poor spy, there's no disguise.
Your heart's as dark as
Theirs was and it speaks
With the same broken accent.

Those flowers, they blossom
Again now, tender buds
Of migraine—souvenirs.
And you call them poems,

Poems with hair slicked back,
Smelling of bay rum, sweat,
And hot buttered popcorn.
Furtive illuminations . . .

for Henri Coulette

Pull down the shades.
Your black boyfriend is coming.
He's not like you. He wants
To live in the suburbs.

You want to paint. Your hand
Does your dreaming for you,
The same hand, braceleted with scars,
That smooths down cats, sheets, men.

Under it your body
Is turning into landscape—look!
Some metamorphosis
Of the moon . . . The ancients

Who watch you from their porches—
You in your earrings, in
Your bare feet, in that long
Boy's undershirt you wear

(Because your breasts are small)—
They're all asleep now,
The insects, the wind . . .
It's late. But then he's married,

And this is still Texas.
The night is a giant cactus.
Potent, aromatic,
The liquors you press from it.

They robbed you of your ticket
To the revolution, oh,
And then they stomped you good.
But nothing stops you.

You have identified yourself
To the police as quote
Lyric poet. What else?—
With fractured jaw. Orpheus,

Imperishable liar!
Your life's a poem still,
Broken iambs and all,
Jazz, jails—the complete works.

And one blue-silver line
Beyond the Antilles,
Vanishing . . . All fragments.
You who could scream across

The square in Cuernavaca,
At a friend you hadn't seen
For years, the one word, *bitch*,
And turn away—that's style!

Or this, your other voice,
This whisper along the wires
At night, like a dry wind,
Like conscience, always collect.

for Robert Boardman Vaughn

The newspaper on the table,
Confessing its lies.
The melon beside it,
Plump, unspoiled,

Trying to forget
That it was ever wrapped up
In anything so
Scandalous, so banal.

Already out, the knife,
Confident lover.
It smiles. It knows
How attractive it is

To sunlight. On the wall,
A guitar, in shadow,
Remembering hands . . .
I don't come into the picture.

Poets, ah, fellow exiles,
It's your scene now, and welcome.
You take up the guitar.
You cut up the melon.

But when are you going to
Roll up the newspaper, swat
The flies, take out all the garbage?
Mañana? Always mañana.

Homage to the Memory of Wallace Stevens

1

Hartford is cold today but no colder for your absence.
The rain is green over Avon and, since your death, the sky
Has been blue many times with a blue you did not imagine.

The judges of Key West sit soberly in black
But only because it is their accustomed garb,
And the sea sings with the same voice still, neither serious nor sorry.

The walls past which you walked in your white suit,
Ponderous, pondering French pictures,
Are no less vivid now. Not one is turned to the wall.

The actuarial tables are not upset.
The mail travels back and forth to Ceylon as before.
The gold leaf peels in season and is renewed.

And there are heroes who falter but do not fall,
Or fall without faltering and without fault,
But you were not one of them. Nevertheless,

The poet practicing his scales
Thinks of you as his thumbs slip clumsily under and under,
Avoiding the darker notes.

2

The *the* has become an *a*. The dictionary
Closed at dusk, along with the zoo in the park.

And the wings of the swans are folded now like the sheets of a long
      letter.
Who borrows your French words and postures now?

3

The opera of the gods is finished,
And the applause is dying.
The chorus will soon be coming down from the clouds.
Even their silence my be understood
As a final platitude of sorts, a summing up.

The tireless dancers have retired at last
To a small apartment on a treeless street.
But, oh, the pas de deux of Eden begins again
On cotsprings creaking like the sun and moon!
The operation of the universe is temporarily suspended.

What has been good? What has been beautiful?
The tuning up, or the being put away?
The instruments have nothing more to say.
Now they will sleep on plush and velvet till
Our breath revives them to new flutterings, new adieux—

And to the picnic all the singers come,
Minus their golden costumes, but no less gods for that.
Now all quotations from the text apply,
Including the laughter, including the offstage thunder,
Including even this almost human cry.

Hartford, 1969

A Letter

You write that you are ill, confused. The trees
Outside the window of the room they gave you
Are wet with tears each morning when they wake you
Out of the sleep you never quite fall into.
There is some dream of traffic in your head

That stops and goes, and goes, and does not stop
Sometimes all night, all day. The motorcade
Winds past you like the funeral cortege
Of someone famous you had slept with, once or twice.
(Another fit of tears dampens the leaves, the page.)

You would expose your wounds, pull down your blouse,
Unbosom yourself wholly to the young doctor
Who has the power to sign prescriptions, passes,
Who seems to like you . . . And so to pass
Into the city once again, one of us,

Hurrying by the damp trees of a park
Towards a familiar intersection where
The traffic signal warns you not to cross,
To wait, just as before, alone—but suddenly
Ten years older, tamed now, less mad, less beautiful.

Three Odes

COOL DARK ODE

You could have sneaked up,
Broken into those underheated rooms
By the windows overlooking the tavern,
Or the back way, up the broad but unlighted stairs,
At a moment when no one was present,
When the long planed table that served as a desk
Was recalling the quiet of the woods,
When the books, older, were thinking farther back,
To the same essential stillness,
And both table and books, if they thought of the future ever,
Probably shuddered, as though from a stray draft,
Seeing themselves as eventual flame,
Some final smoke.

Now, when there is no longer any occasion,
I think of inviting you in
To wait for us
On the short, cramped sofa,
Beside the single candle-stub
Which must have frightened you off then,
Or in the cubicle of the bedroom,
Where even then we imagined ourselves extinguished
By your total embrace,
Attentive meanwhile to the animal noises of your breathing,
The whimpers,
The sudden intoxicated outcries,
That were not our own.

Night, night, O blackness of winter,
I tell you this, you
That used to come up as far as the frosted panes, the door,
As far as the edges of our skin,
Without any thought, I know now,
Of entering those borrowed rooms,
Or even our mouths, our eyes,
Which all too often were carelessly left open for you.

It was still possible then
To imagine that no more than one or two hands
Would ever move down the face of the hour,
And that the shadow which followed
Might remain patient
And, if anything, somewhat reluctant to continue;
That no more than one or two hands
Had ever descended so far
As the shoulders of the afternoon,
And that, necessarily, they would have been bare then
Of even that shadow which, sometimes, the air itself seems to be
    charged with
And to suffer from;
That no more than one or two hands surely
Would have crossed the forbidden zone
At the end of summer,
And that the sky there would be turning always from white to pink,
    slowly,
And that it could no longer matter then
What shadows rose from your hollows and sank back.

And it is still possible to imagine
That there are one or two hands
Which do not know, or which do not yet know,
Anything of either that face or the shadow
Which does, after all, follow,
Or of flushed shoulders or turning sky,
Or of those particular hollows, alive
With less and less curious and impulsive shadows now;
And that there may somewhere be hands
Which will never be smeared with the very special pollen
And general muskiness of a dying summer;
And that there are probably other hands which have stopped,
Or will stop, or even now are shaken with premonitions
Of a time when they will have begun to stop,
And among these some which remember little or nothing
Of you and your coloring,
And some also which do not and cannot forget
Your blood upon them and your dew.

Not with the vague smoke
In the curtains,
Not with the pigeons or doves
Under the eaves,
Nevertheless you are there, hidden,
And again you wake me,
Scentless, noiseless,
Someone or something,
Something or someone faithless,
And that will not return.

Undiscovered star,
That fade and are fading,
Fixed,
And that will not return.

Someone, someone or something,
Colorless, formless,
And that will not return.

The Telephone Number of the Muse

Sleepily, the muse to me: 'Let us be friends.
Good friends, but only friends.   You understand.'
And yawned.   And kissed, for the last time, my ear.
Who earlier, weeping at my touch, had whispered:
'I loved you once.'   And: 'No, I don't love him.
Not after everything he did.'   Later,
Rebuttoning her nightgown with my help:
'Sorry, I just have no desire, it seems.'
Sighing: 'For you, I mean.'   Long silence.   Then:
'You always were so serious.'   At which
I smiled, darkly.   And that was how I came
To sleep beside, not with her; without dreams.

I call her up sometimes, long distance now.
And she still knows my voice, but I can hear,
Beyond the music of her phonograph,
The laughter of the young men with their keys.

I have the number written down somewhere.

White Notes

1

Suddenly there was a dress,
Inhabited, in motion.

It contained a forest,
Small birds, rivers.

It contained the ivory
Of piano keys,
White notes.

Across the back of a chair
Skins of animals
Dried in the moon.

2

It happened.
Your body went out of your body.

It rose
To let the air in,
The night.

From the sheets it rose,
From the bare floor,
Floating.

Over roofs,
Smaller and smaller,
Lost.

Entangled now
In the cold arms
Of distant street lamps.

3

The city forgets where you live.
It wanders through many streets,
And the streets turn, confused,
Upon one another.

Parks have deserted themselves.
All night, awnings are whipped
And cannot remember.

O forgotten umbrella . . .
Darkness saw you, air
Displaced you, words
Erased you.

4

And afterwards,
After the quenching of the street lamps,
Long after the ivory could have been brought back to life by any
    touch.

Afterwards, when I might have told you
The address of your future.
Long after the future.

When the umbrella had been closed forever.
Then, when not even the moon
Would have the power to bruise you any more.

Then, in another time.

An Elegy Is Preparing Itself

There are pines that are tall enough
Already. In the distance,
The whining of saws; and needles,
Silently slipping through the chosen cloth.
The stone, then as now, unfelt,
Perfectly weightless. And certain words,
That will come together to mourn,
Waiting, in their dark clothes, apart.

From a Notebook

1

Named ambassador
To the High Court of Prose,
I neglect my manners, my dress,
Speak in a loud voice, at length,
And am everywhere taken
For one of the natives.

2

Novelist and naturalist,
P. turns to poetry
In search, once more,
Of the true primitive.

May he locate the tribe,
Master the dialect.

3

Though, as G. says,
We American poets
No longer love words,
It is hard not to remember
What we felt for
Those that betrayed us,
Those we betrayed.

4

The Texas millionaire
Offered to give the Church
Ten thousand dollars
In exchange for her virtue.

Advised by the priest
To follow her conscience,
She gave up
Working for charity.

5
Jesus Christ Superstar
Favors us with a performance
Of one of his poems,

Purporting to describe
The virtues of elephant oil
As applied to the tips of the mammaries.

6
FROM A SPY NOVEL: "Maybe you know Bliss by another name."

7
AFTER THE CHINESE (I)

Near the summit,
They rest on separate rocks, smoking,
And wonder whether the wildflowers
Are worth going on for.

8
After the overture,
The opera seemed brief.

9
WORKSHOP

G. maintains that the Adjective somehow penetrates the Noun with all that is most private, thereby becoming the most Personal of the Parts of Speech, hence the most Beautiful.

I, on the contrary, maintain that the Conjunction, being Impersonal, is the more Beautiful, and especially when suppressed.

10
M., opening my diary, found the pages blank.

11

AFTER THE CHINESE (II)

Discs for a cough,
A smooth stone for remembrance.

And the man in the old song,
For a single quince out of season,
Sent back a poem that lasted
Three thousand years.

Variations on a Text by Vallejo

Me moriré en París con aguacero . . .

I will die in Miami in the sun,
On a day when the sun is very bright,
A day like the days I remember, a day like other days,
A day that nobody knows or remembers yet,
And the sun will be bright then on the dark glasses of strangers
And in the eyes of a few friends from my childhood
And of the surviving cousins by the graveside,
While the diggers, standing apart, in the still shade of the palms,
Rest on their shovels, and smoke,
Speaking in Spanish softly, out of respect.

I think it will be on a Sunday like today,
Except that the sun will be out, the rain will have stopped,
And the wind that today made all the little shrubs kneel down;
And I think it will be a Sunday because today,
When I took out this paper and began to write,
Never before had anything looked so blank,
My life, these words, the paper, the gray Sunday;
And my dog, quivering under a table because of the storm,
Looked up at me, not understanding,
And my son read on without speaking, and my wife slept.

Donald Justice is dead. One Sunday the sun came out,
It shone on the bay, it shone on the white buildings,
The cars moved down the street slowly as always, so many,
Some with their headlights on in spite of the sun,
And after a while the diggers with their shovels
Walked back to the graveside through the sunlight,
And one of them put his blade into the earth
To lift a few clods of dirt, the black marl of Miami,
And scattered the dirt, and spat,
Turning away abruptly, out of respect.

Absences

It's snowing this afternoon and there are no flowers.
There is only this sound of falling, quiet and remote,
Like the memory of scales descending the white keys
Of a childhood piano—outside the window, palms!
And the heavy head of the cereus, inclining,
Soon to let down its white or yellow-white.

Now, only these poor snow-flowers in a heap,
Like the memory of a white dress cast down . . .
So much has fallen.
                    And I, who have listened for a step
All afternoon, hear it now, but already falling away,
Already in memory. And the terrible scales descending
On the silent piano; the snow; and the absent flowers abounding.

Presences

Everyone, everyone went away today.
They left without a word, and I think
I did not hear a single goodbye today.

And all that I saw was someone's hand, I think,
Thrown up out there like the hand of someone drowning,
But far away, too far to be sure what it was or meant.

No, but I saw how everything had changed
Later, just as the light had; and at night
I saw that from dream to dream everything changed.

And those who might have come to me in the night,
The ones who did come back but without a word,
All those I remembered passed through my hands like clouds—

Clouds out of the south, familiar clouds—
But I could not hold onto them, they were drifting away,
Everything going away in the night again and again.

Sonatina in Green

One spits on the sublime.
One lies in bed alone, reading
Yesterday's newspaper. One
Has composed a beginning, say,
A phrase or two. No more!
There has been traffic enough
In the boudoir of the muse.

And still they come, demanding entrance,
Noisy, and with ecstatic cries
Catching the perfume, forcing their way—
For them, what music? Only,
Distantly, through some door ajar,
Echoes, broken strains; and the garland
Crushed at the threshold.

                And we,
We few with the old instruments,
Obstinate, sounding the one string—
For us, what music? Only, at times,
The sunlight of late afternoon
That plays in the corner of a room,
Playing upon worn keys. At times,
Smells of decaying greenery, faint bouquets—
More than enough.

              And our cries
Diminish behind us:
                Cover
The bird cages! No more
Bargain days in the flower stalls!
There has been traffic enough
In the boudoir of the muse,
More than enough traffic. Or say
That one composed, in the end,
Another beginning, in spite of all this,
Sublime. Enough!

Closed are the grand boulevards,
And closed those mouths that made the lesser songs,
And the curtains drawn in the boudoir.

for my students

Sonatina in Yellow

Du schnell vergehendes Daguerrotyp
In meinen langsamer vergehenden Händen.
                                                    RILKE

The pages of the album,
As they are turned, turn yellow; a word,
Once spoken, obsolete,
No longer what was meant. Say it.
The meanings come, or come back later,
Unobtrusive, taking their places.

Think of the past. Think of forgetting the past.
It was an exercise requiring further practice;
A difficult exercise, played through by someone else.
Overheard from another room, now,
It seems full of mistakes.
                              So the voice of your father,
Rising as from the next room still
With all the remote but true affection of the dead,
Repeats itself, insists,
Insisting you must listen, rises
In the familiar pattern of reproof
For some childish error, a nap disturbed,
Or vase, broken or overturned;
Rises and subsides. And you do listen.
Listen and forget. Practice forgetting.

Forgotten sunlight still
Blinds the eyes of faces in the album.
The faces fade, and there is only
A sort of meaning that comes back,
Or for the first time comes, but comes too late
To take the places of the faces.

                              Remember
The dead air of summer. Remember
The trees drawn up to their full height like fathers,
The underworld of shade you entered at their feet.
Enter the next room. Enter it quietly now,
Not to disturb your father sleeping there. *He stirs.*
Notice his clothes, how scrupulously clean,

Unwrinkled from the nap; his face, freckled with work,
Smoothed by a passing dream. The vase
Is not yet broken, the still young roses
Drink there from perpetual waters. *He rises, speaks* . . .

Repeat it now, no one was listening.
So your hand moves, moving across the keys,
And slowly the keys grow darker to the touch.

Riddle

White of a blind man's eye
I saw rolling.
When the lid closed over,
Dark was twice dark.

Soon I saw glitter
His other eye.
Dew fell then; dark scattered.
What it saw, men saw.

(THE MOON AND THE SUN)

for Stephen Dobyns

UNCOLLECTED
POEMS

Sonnet: An Old-Fashioned Devil

Tu le connais, lecteur, ce monstre délicat . . .
BAUDELAIRE

Who is it snarls our plow lines, wastes our fields,
Unbaits our hooks, and fishes out our streams?
Who leads our hunts to where the good earth yields
To marshlands, and we sink, but no one screams?
Who taught our children where the harlot lives?
They gnaw her nipples and they drain her pap,
Clapping their little hands like primitives
With droll abandon, bouncing on her lap.
Our wives adore him; us he bores to tears.
Who cares if to our dry and yellow grass
He strikes a match or two, then disappears?
It's only the devil on his flop-eared ass—
A beast too delicate to bear him well—
Come plodding by us on his way to hell.

Summer, 1948

111

The Return of Alcestis

HERCULES

I bring Alcestis from the dolorous shades.

ADMETUS

Ah, what can ail her? She neither weeps nor smiles.

ALCESTIS

My latest sighs have somewhat scorched the veil.
Ah, what can ail me? I neither weep nor smile.
Why has he brought me from the dolorous shades?

1950

Two Songs from Don Juan in Hell

1 SGANARELLE'S SONG

The gardens are golden with leaves,
Notes drawn on the season's Exchange;
But my purse is as limp as the sleeves
That amputees learn to arrange.

> *No, no, nothing assuages*
> *The pains of damnation*
> *Like regular wages*
> *And a two-weeks' vacation.*

The sun and the moon are as bright
As coins that collectors collect.
But why should my purse be so light
With no sun for the moon to reflect?

> *No, no, nothing assuages, etc.*

2 DON JUAN'S SONG

The devil's like a jealous, jealous husband,
But I must blame his horns upon another.
Oh, evil's like a young wife from the country,
Approachable, but hardly worth the bother.

Damnation's like an heiress, much proposed to.
Why has she chosen me to be her groom?
Hell is a cheap hotel, if continental:
The bridal suite is just a small, hot room.

1953

113

The Summer Anniversaries

At ten I was wheeled in a chair
Past vacant lots in bloom
With goldenrod and with broom,
And all the yards in flower,
The simple voice of a bird
Or a housewife from her yard
Flowering in my ear,
Until I thought it absurd
For anyone to have quarreled
Ever with such a world—
O brave new planet!—
And with such music in it.

At twenty or twenty-one
I stood in a bustling park
On the lower East Side of New York
And watched a child's balloon,
Released, veer crazily off,
Comparing it to myself,
All sense of direction gone;
And the melancholy F
Of an East River tug,
Groping its way through the fog,
With each repeated blast
Reminded me I was lost.

At thirty now I watch
Through the window beside my desk
Boys deep in the summer dusk
Of Iowa, at catch,
Toss, back and forth, their ball.
Shadows begin to fall.
The colors of the day
Resolve into one dull,
Unremarkable gray,
And I watch them go in from their play,
Small figures of some myth
Now, vanishing up the path.

1955

From *Bad Dreams*

EPILOGUE: TO THE MORNING LIGHT

O light,
Strike out across the pasture,
Where nightmare runs away now,
Unseating all her riders.
Show them the way through woods where
So recently they wandered,
Without direction. Shine, shine on those spiders'
Webs into which they blundered,
So many, recoiling with a gesture.

Dazzle the highways, paved
With fading journeys. And these walks
That lead into a town
From which the siege is lifting
Lace, lace with leaf-pattern now
Through the cooperation of the oaks
And breezes constantly shifting.

Then leap the latched gate lightly,
O prodigal. Approach
This house, this anxious house your nightly
Exile fills with gloom. How many chores
Await you! It is to you the stories
Declare themselves, all three now,
And at your glance how whitely!

Look in through the tinted oval,
There where the stair turns. No longer
Delay your necessary arrival.
But quickly, quickly
Stoop to the frayed runner
And follow it up the stair—
Steep, but less dangerous now that you
Go with it everywhere.

And reward every sleeper
With waking, with forgetting,
Your brilliant trophies.
Raise them up but with care
From pallets now and sofas,
Where they have hung suspended
Over abysms, chasms,
Or drifted deep and deeper
Down through lost, bottomless pools.
See that their dreams are ended.

Teach them to forgive the mirror
Its frank, unfaltering look,
And the sundial in the side yard
Its shadow, for your sake,
For only with your help shall
They come to see—and with no more
Than average daily terror—
All things for what they are.

1959

The Furies

One is a bitch with stinking
Fur matted with dung.
Kicked and pampered in turn,
Always it comes slinking
Bellywise after you
With damp muzzle, with tongue,
Beseeching some favor whose
Nature you never learn.
       This one is dangerous

Another rides your shoulder
Like any seaman's parrot,
Only its tongue is bolder.
No pet bird to be proud of,
It will rail and swear at
You seven days running out of
Mere avian pique
And rake at you with its beak.
       Some find this useful

The last resembles a mirror
With this one curious trick,
That it is blank always.
Where do you go then when you
Look therein? What hallways
Keep you? By what error
Is the great avenue
Suddenly emptied of its traffic?
       Avoid this one

for certain reviewers

1962

Little Elegy

Weep, all you girls
Who prize good looks and song.
Mack, the canary, is dead.

A girl very much like you
Kept him by her twelve months
Close as a little brother.

He perched where he pleased,
Hopped, chirping, from breast to breast,
And fed, sometimes, pecking from her mouth.

O lucky bird! But death
Plucks from the air even
The swiftest, the most favored.

Red are the eyes of his mistress now.
On us, her remaining admirers,
They do not yet quite focus.

After Catullus

118

First Death

JUNE 12, 1933

I saw my grandmother grow weak.
When she died, I kissed her cheek.

I remember the new taste—
Powder mixed with a drying paste.

Down the hallway, on its table,
Lay the family's great Bible.

In the dark, by lamplight stirred,
The Void grew pregnant with the Word.

In black ink they wrote it down.
The older ink was turning brown.

From the woods there came a cry—
The hoot owl asking who, not why.

The men sat silent on the porch,
Each lighted pipe a friendly torch

Against the unknown and the known.
But the child knew himself alone.

JUNE 13, 1933

The morning sun rose up and stuck.
Sunflower strove with hollyhock.

I ran the worn path past the sty.
Nothing was hidden from God's eye.

The barn door creaked. I walked among
Chaff and wrinkled cakes of dung.

In the dim light I read the dates
On the dusty license plates

Nailed to the wall as souvenirs.
I breathed the dust in of the years.

I circled the abandoned Ford
Before I tried the running board.

At the wheel I felt the heat
Press upwards through the springless seat.

And when I touched the silent horn,
Small mice scattered through the corn.

JUNE 14, 1933

I remember the soprano
Fanning herself at the piano,

And the preacher looming large
Above me in his dark blue serge.

My shoes brought in a smell of clay
To mingle with the faint sachet

Of flowers sweating in their vases.
A stranger showed us to our places.

The stiff fan stirred in mother's hand.
Air moved, but only when she fanned.

I wondered how could all her grief
Be squeezed into one small handkerchief.

There was a buzzing on the sill.
It stopped, and everything was still.

We bowed our heads, we closed our eyes
To the mercy of the flies.

Two Blues

1   THE SOMETIME DANCER BLUES

When the lights go on uptown,
Why do you feel so low, honey,
Why do you feel so low-down?

When the piano and the trombone start,
Why do you feel so blue, honey,
Like a rubber glove had reached in for your heart?

Oh, when the dancers take the floor,
Why don't you step on out, honey,
Why won't you step out with them anymore?

The stars are gone and the night is dark,
Except for the radium, honey,
That glows on the hands of the bedside clock,

The little hands that go around and around,
Oh, as silently as time, honey,
Without a sound, without a sound.

A dark time is coming, and the gypsy knows what else.
Fly away, O angel death.

It looks like a raven sitting on the wire.
It looks like a raven sitting on the telephone wire.
Oh, it is some high flyer!

Look out now, it's got loose in the yard.
Look out, look out, it's loose in the back yard.
Oh, no, don't you look at me, big bird.

If you are lost, I can't help.
If you are lost, I can't help.
I am a stranger in this place myself.

Fly away, fly away,
Fly away, O angel death.

And shine down, moonlight, make those long feathers shine.
I want to keep track of where it's going.
(*Spoken*) Shine down, moonlight.

Tremayne

Snow melting and the dog
Barks lonely on his bottom from the yard.
The ground is frozen but not hard.

The seasonal and vague
Despairs of February settle over
Tremayne now like a light snow cover,

And he sits thinking; sits
Also not thinking for a while of much.
So February turns to March.

Snow turns to rain; a hyacinth
Pokes up; doves returning moan and sing.
Tremayne takes note of one more spring—

Mordancies of the armchair!—
And finds it hard not to be reconciled
To a despair that seems so mild.

Tremayne stands in the sunlight,
        Watering his lawn.
The sun seems not to move at all,
        Till it has moved on.

The twilight sounds commence now
        As those of water cease,
And he goes barefoot through the stir,
        Almost at peace.

Light leans in pale rectangles
        Out against the night.
Tremayne asks nothing more now. There's
        Just enough light,

Or when the street lamp catches
        There should be. He pauses:
How simple it all seems for once!—
        These sidewalks, these still houses.

Unflushed Urinals

lines written in the Omaha bus station

Seeing them, I recognize the contempt
Some men have for themselves.

This man, for instance, zipping quickly up, head turned,
Like a bystander innocent of his own piss.

And here comes one to repair himself at the mirror,
Patting down damp, sparse hairs, suspiciously still black,
Poor bantam cock of a man, jaunty at one a.m., perfumed,
          undiscourageable . . .

O the saintly forbearance of these mirrors!
The acceptingness of the washbowls, in which we absolve ourselves!

Sunday Afternoon in Buffalo, Texas

bus stop, 4:30 p.m.

Four or five roads converge here, going somewhere else.

And on the concrete apron of the Conoco station
This boy all afternoon has practiced squealing his new radials
With the sound of a young giantess repeatedly climaxing.

One carload of the converted, dressed for evening service,
Parks on thin grass beside the highway—nothing to do
But watch us stumble, thirsty and disheveled, down the bus steps.

The Buffalo Flower Shop is closed; on its door
The little paper clock is set for tomorrow. But I
Will dream tonight of the wild buffalo flower, O rare and shaggy!

Leaving town, we pass a yard made colorful
By red and yellow flowerpots strung between trees,
Like lanterns left on after some long and marvellous party.

Population: One-Two-Four-Two . . .

Memories of the Depression Years

1   A FARM NEAR TIFTON, GEORGIA, C. 1930

. . . in the kitchen, as she bends to serve,
Aunt Babe's too finely thin, upgathered hair
Filters the sunlight coming through behind
(Which is how Griffith lights his heroines).
Moth-wings cling to the door-screen; dust-motes whirl.
There is such a light!
                    The grown-ups chatter on,
Unheard. Meanwhile I listen for the freight,
Due any minute. I can *see* the bell
Swing back and forth in close-up, silently,
The huge wheels revolving, the steam rising . . .
But already the silent world is lost forever.

2   BOSTON, GEORGIA, C. 1933

The tin roofs catch the slanting sunlight.
A few cows turn homeward up back lanes;
Boys with sticks nudge the cattle along.
A pickup whines past. The dust rises.
Crows call; cane sweetens along the stalk;
All around, soundlessly, gnats hover.
And from his stoop now my grandfather
Stands watching as all this comes to pass.

3   MIAMI, FLORIDA, C. 1936

Our new house on the edge of town
Looks bare at first, and raw. A pink
Plaster flamingo on one leg
Stands preening by the lily pond.
And just as the sun begins to sink
Into the Everglades beyond,
It seems to shatter against the pane
In little asterisks of light,
And on our lids half-closed in prayer
Over the clean blue willowware.

In the Attic

There's a half hour towards dusk when flies,
Trapped by the summer screens, expire
Musically in the dust of sills;
And ceilings slope towards remembrance.

The same crimson afternoons expire
Over the same few rooftops repeatedly;
Only, being stored up for remembrance,
They somehow escape the ordinary.

Childhood is like that, repeatedly
Lost in the very longueurs it redeems.
One forgets how small and ordinary
The world looked once by dusklight from above . . .

But not the moment which redeems
The drowsy arias of the flies—
And the chin settles onto palms above
Numbed elbows propped on rotting sills.

Thinking about the Past

Certain moments will never change, nor stop being—
My mother's face all smiles, all wrinkles soon;
The rock wall building, built, collapsed then, fallen;
Our upright loosening downward slowly out of tune—
All fixed into place now, all rhyming with each other.
That red-haired girl with wide mouth—Eleanor—
Forgotten thirty years—her freckled shoulders, hands.
The breast of Mary Something, freed from a white swimsuit,
Damp, sandy, warm; or Margery's, a small, caught bird—
Darkness they rise from, darkness they sink back toward.
O marvellous early cigarettes! O bitter smoke, Benton . . .
And Kenny in wartime whites, crisp, cocky,
Time a bow bent with his certain failure.
Dusks, dawns; waves; the ends of songs . . .

Childhood

J'ai heurté, savez-vous, d'incroyables Florides . . .
RIMBAUD

TIME: *the thirties*
PLACE: *Miami, Florida*

Once more beneath my thumb the globe turns—
And doomed republics pass in a blur of colors . . .

            Winter mornings now, my grandfather,
Head bared to the mild sunshine, likes to spread
The Katzenjammers out around a white lawn chair
To catch the stray curls of citrus from his knife.
Chameleons quiver in ambush; wings
Of monarchs beat above bronze turds, feasting . . .
                And there are pilgrim ants
Eternally bearing incommensurate crumbs
Past slippered feet. —There,
In the lily pond, my own face wrinkles
With the slow teasings of a stick.
              The long days pass, days
Streaked with the colors of the first embarrassments . . .
And Sundays, among kin, happily ignored,
I sit nodding, somnolent with horizons:
              Myriad tiny suns
Drown in the deep mahogany polish of the chair-arms;
Bunched cushions prickle through starched cotton . . .
                  Already
I know the pleasure of certain solitudes.
I can look up at a ceiling so theatrical
Its stars seem more aloof than the real stars;
And pre-depression putti blush in the soft glow
Of exit signs. Often I blink, re-entering
The world—or catch, surprised, in a shop window,
My ghostly image skimming across nude mannequins.
Drawbridges, careless of traffic, lean there
Against the low clouds—early evening . . .

Czechoslovakia, e.g.

The Katzenjammer Kids—for some years the feature comic strip of the Sunday Miami Herald

the Olympia Theater

                                        All day
There is a smell of ocean longing landward.
And, high on his frail ladder, my father
Stands hammering great storm shutters down
Across the windows of the tall hotels,
Swaying. Around downed wires, across broken fronds,
Our Essex steers, bargelike and slow . . .
                        Westward now,
The smoky rose of oblivion blooms, hangs;
And on my knee a small red sun-glow, setting.
For a long time I feel, coming and going in waves,
The stupid wish to cry. I dream . . .
                                And there are
Colognes that mingle on the barber's hands
Swathing me in his striped cloth Saturdays, downtown.
Billy, the midget haberdasher, stands grinning
Under the winking neon goat, his sign—
And Flagler's sidewalks fill. Slowly
The South's first escalator rattles upward
Towards the twin fountains of a mezzanine
Where boys, secretly brave, prepare to taste
The otherness trickling there, forbidden . . .
And then the warm cashews in cool arcades!
O counters of spectacles!—where the bored child first
Scans new perspectives squinting through strange lenses;
And the mirrors, tilting, offer back toy sails
Stiffening breezeless towards green shores of baize . . .

                How thin the grass looks of the new yards—
                        And everywhere
The fine sand burning into the bare heels
With which I learn to crush, going home,
The giant sandspurs of the vacant lots.
Iridescences of mosquito hawks
Glimmer above brief puddles filled with skies,
Tropical and changeless. And sometimes,
Where the city halts, the cracked sidewalks
Lead to a coral archway still spanning
The entrance to some wilderness of palmetto—

Forlorn suburbs, but with golden names!

134

the hurricane season

obsolete make of car

the Everglades on fire
my osteomyelitis—anesthesias

the Capitol Barber Shop—M. DuPree, proprietor

Billy's Men's Shop

the principal east-west street
in Cromer-Cassell's (later Richards') Department Store.
the shameful 'white' and 'colored' drinking fountains of those days
and that region—against which we reacted in our own way

the 5-and 10¢ stores—a tray of unsorted eyeglasses in Grant's—a toy
display in Woolworth's

the N.W. section, still under development

Sunny Isles, Golden Glades, Buena Vista, Opa-Locka, etc.

> *—Dedicated to the poets of a mythical childhood—*
> *Wordsworth, Rimbaud, Hart Crane, and Alberti*

Notes

Poems included here from earlier volumes are arranged in fair chronological order. Poems previously uncollected follow their own separate chronological arrangement, and to the earliest of these I have added dates, since I often find myself curious about such things in the work of others. One of the pleasures of working on this book lay in trying to improve poems I found it hard either to abandon or to stand by. As a result, many are here revised, some in no more than punctuation, some in word or phrase, and several somewhat more thoroughly.

———

Most of the details in *A Dancer's Life* were remembered, perhaps wrongly, from early Bergman movies, scripts, and criticism.

The Confession, The Success, The Assassination, and, to some extent, the two sonatinas come in part from chance methods.

The last section of *Homage to the Memory of Wallace Stevens* refers to a libretto I supplied for Edward Miller's opera, *The Young God*, to its performance and to the accompanying celebrations, which took place in Hartford in the spring of 1969. Line 22 is meant to echo a famous line from *Lycidas*.

The structure of *Cool Dark Ode* is modeled loosely on that of part iv of Rafael Alberti's *Colegio (S.J.)*. Several lines in *White Notes* were suggested by passages scattered through his *Sobres los ángeles*.

Riddle is based on a well-known Old English riddle.

Don Juan in Hell was to have been a puppet opera, based on the Baudelaire poem.

Bad Dreams was to have been composed mostly of the dreams dreamed by the kinspeople gathered together in the house of the head of the family during the night on which he lay dying. Some debt for the idea undoubtedly was owed to James Agee and to Peter Taylor, perhaps even to Dylan Thomas, but I can no longer judge how much.

#2 of *Memories of the Depression Years* (Boston, Georgia) is a kind of *imitation* of the Wang Wei poem which has been translated as *A Farm-House on the Wei River*. #3 (Miami, Florida) is similarly related to Baudelaire's *Je n'ai pas oublié* . . .

Donald Justice

Donald Justice was born in Miami, Florida, in 1925 and grew up there. After attending the University of Miami, he studied at the University of North Carolina, Stanford, and Iowa. He has taught at a number of universities, including Syracuse and the University of California (Irvine), as well as Iowa, where he now teaches. His first book, *The Summer Anniversaries*, was the Lamont poetry selection for 1959. He has also published *Night Light* (1967), *Departures* (1973) and was the editor of *The Collected Poems of Weldon Kees* (1960) and co-editor, with Alexander Aspel, of *Contemporary French Poetry* (1965). He has received grants in poetry from The Rockefeller Foundation, The Guggenheim Foundation and the National Council on the Arts, and in theater from The Ford Foundation. He is married and has one son, Nathaniel.